PUT YOUR MOUTH ON IT

Speak Life to Your Next Level of
Wealth, Success and Happiness

Rynette Upson-Bush

ILLUMINATION PRESS

Atlanta, Georgia

PUT YOUR MOUTH ON IT
Speak Life to Your Next Level of Wealth, Success, and Happiness
Copyright © 2019 by Rynette Upson-Bush

ISBN: 978-1-950681-01-3
Cover and Interior Design by AugustPride, LLC
ILLUMINATION Press
1100 Peachtree Street
Suite 250
Atlanta, Georgia 30309
United States

CONTENTS

DEDICATION

This book is dedicated to:

Every person who has allowed negativity and the negative words spoken over them to hold them back. Don't believe those lies! That's not who you are!

My parents, William and Carolyn Upson—you always did the best you knew to do and always gave your all Thank you! I love you both so much!

My children, Trace, Chris, AJ, Michael, Brittany, Quiniesha and Niki, who are now learning to use the power of their mouth to manifest their dreams. You shall possess what you confess! Put your mouth on it! I love y'all so much!

Revel, JJ you have shown me the power of my own words. You encouraged me so many times and you didn't even know it. Love you!

My husband, Angel, who is my angel sent straight from Heaven. I killed your dreams because I didn't know better at the time but you supported me and my dreams every time. I just want to say thank you for always being there! Forever in love with you!

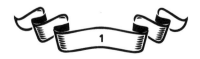

ACKNOWLEDGEMENTS

Dr. James and Dr. Stacia Pierce—you changed my life and introduced me to a whole new world, a world I never knew. You taught me the power of positive thinking. You spoke so many positive words over me and my family. Your difference has made me different and I thank God for placing you all in my life! I'm forever grateful. Much love, honor, and respect!

Dr. Riva Tims—thank you for always being an example of how to put your mouth on your dreams and never give up no matter what you're going through. Your strength has been a true example in my life. Much love, honor, and respect.

To my dear friends...

Robert Alston • Carole Davis • Janese Hammonds • Pontressa Mitchner • Angel Richards

Thank you all for the constant words of encouragement, your support and for always being there. My brother and my sisters not by blood but through love and life. My push team... I love y'all to life!

I must acknowledge my Creator, the King of all Kings, the God of all gods—it's only because of You that this is a reality and that my life is what it is today. Thank You for choosing me when I didn't even know how to choose myself. Your name will forever be in my heart and in my mouth! God, l love You forever!

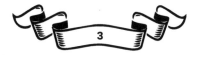

INTRODUCTION

It took me a long time to really understand that my mouth was the source of many of my frustrations. I spent many years longing and looking for my bright future to arrive, but it never did.

I prayed and got excited many times after hearing sermons at church. I was hopeful but not fully believing. I thought there could be a small possibility of things working out for me. I would come out of church saying, "I hope things don't go wrong this time."

Many times, it seemed like everything got worse instead of better. I would see some successes but, in the end, things never really worked out for me. For years, I felt alone. I was broke, busted, and disgusted. My marriage was a mess—baby daddy drama. I had three jobs— two that I loved, but they didn't pay enough, and one that didn't pay enough, and I hated it. I was entrenched in family dissension and I was surrounded by a circle of friends who were just like me. I was constantly focused on what was wrong and not doing much to change it. Never looking at the good, always focused on the bad. Going through life accepting what it gave me instead of creating what I wanted was my norm.

Yep, that's how I lived, but nobody really knew. I always looked good on the outside, but I was jacked up on the inside because of

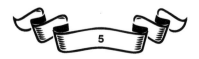

negative words that people spoke over me and ones I spoke over myself. The sad part is—I believed the negativity. I accepted what was said to me and about me. I believed it all to be true. I would always pray and hope for the best, but I never really thought it would happen for me. Honestly, it seemed like prayer was a waste of time. I stayed confused about why my dream seemed to be just a dream that would never come to reality. I worked and fought hard for what I believed I should have. I went to church and believed in God and prayed for better days, but it seemed like I just couldn't get ahead for some reason. I felt really confused about why God kept overlooking me.

Truthfully, I used to actually be mad at God for putting me in such a position. I was what I call a public success but a private failure.

Maybe you can relate. What I didn't understand at that time was I used my words and the words of others to keep myself stuck, stale, and stagnant. My prayers weren't going to work because I didn't really believe good stuff could happen for me. Even though I believed in God, I didn't believe in me. I didn't know that I was using my mouth to kill my purpose and every dream I had. Most things that came out of my mouth were negative and if I did say something positive, I would come behind the positive with a negative and negate all the good I confessed before it.

Unhappy, unsatisfied and unfulfilled, living in a never ending negative spiral, I knew something in me had to change if I was going to walk in my purpose and realize my dreams. I always had dreams, and big dreams at that, but I never believed them. When I did believe a little bit that my dream could come true by the time I shared my dream with someone, it was usually killed and confirmed that I was thinking too big, doing too much or being extra.

One day something woke me up and made me decide it was truly time for me to walk in my truth. I realized I needed to work on me. It was a lot to swallow, but it was necessary for my life to change. I just knew there was more for me. I knew there were new levels I was supposed to reach. I just knew that I had a purpose. It was time for CHANGE!

It didn't happen overnight, but when I decided to put my mouth on what God said and stopped using my mouth to contribute to my own carcinogenic behavior, chaotic and confusion filled drama, my entire life changed and that's when I was able to take my life in a new direction and to new levels I never knew or thought were possible.

But, do you want to know when my life really changed? It was when I changed my circle. When I got around positive people and they were speaking of manifesting dreams and using your mouth to produce what you wanted to see in life. This was very strange to me at first, and I actually felt it was cultish. I met these very positive people when I switched churches. They were overly friendly, very complimentary and really helpful. This was so weird and different, but in a good way. My negative thinking kept creeping in every time I got around this group of women at church. I even thought to myself, "They are phony. They are just way too positive." They invited me to different outings, but I would always refuse. I was used to the negative and was taught to think that way. This was a way of protecting me from a cruel world and from disappointments in life. If I looked at the negative, I didn't have to get hurt when things didn't go my way. Early in life, my mother taught me to never trust anyone but family. She taught me to never get too close to anyone because people were just users and losers. After all, research has shown about 80 percent of people's thoughts are negative and I was definitely in the 80 percent.

One day, one of the women invited me to a women's conference. This conference was not sponsored by the church, but it was focused on manifesting your dreams and the power of positive thinking. This conference was huge, with women from all over the United States and Bahamas. I met several more women with the same positive vibe as the women at my church. It was actually refreshing! This conference was a real game changer for me!

I started to believe that I could really manifest anything I wanted. I ventured to even think I could start my own school and leave the school system. I told my sister of the idea, and, to my surprise, she was actually on board. She was tired of her job with the school system too. She was excited about manifesting this dream of having our own business. We had been talking about a business before I went to this conference, but the conference gave me a whole new excitement. My sister and I made a pact—we would definitely open a school in the near future. Because we were used to people being negative, we decided to keep our dreams and plans secret until we were further along in the process. When we did start to tell people, we knew they were negative and not supportive at all, but that didn't matter to me because I had a new circle of positive friends and a church family who believed in me and my dreams.

My talk started to change! My actions started to change and my whole life of being negative and never manifesting what I said began to change because I spoke positive words and actually believed them! My marriage started to come together. I was so excited and so passionate about my new walk and my new talk I decided to start a women's empowerment business to teach women how to emerge to their destiny.

In September 2012—eight months after changing my circle and

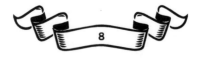

putting my mouth on the positive—I walked away from my career of seventeen years on a quest to open my school.

It wasn't as easy as I thought, but I made up my mind to continue my faith walk and there was no turning back. My goal was to find a building and start the school by January 2013. Unfortunately, things did not go as I planned.

We found what we thought was the perfect building and invested a lot of money in renovations. A few weeks into the project, my sister and I were devastated to learn that the county wouldn't approve our plans. We went before the board, rallied friends to plead our case, but we were denied again. I felt like my world was over for a minute, but I was determined to stay positive and put my mouth on the fact that my school would open. I cried and prayed for about two days, then I got myself together and went on the hunt for another building.

Within a week, I found a new location. I called in my architect, engineer, and contractor again. We had the plans drawn up again. We also had the Department of Children and Family Services come out to inspect the building to see if it would be a go. Everything was falling in place. I put down $25,000 for the deposit on a Friday and was supposed to get the keys the following Monday, but when Monday came, I heard absolutely nothing from the realty company. When I finally got in contact with the realtor, he told me the anchor store in the plaza didn't want a school in the building but he was going to speak to the corporate office and get everything handled. After three weeks of silence from my realtor, I demanded my money back and had to threaten to get an attorney before I received a response. It was a month before I finally got my money back. And, once again I was back to square one. Through all of this, I surprisingly still believed I would find the right building for the school.

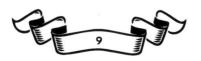

As I began to look for the third building, I stayed positive. I kept believing. I kept saying, "God, please give us the right building, the right size and the right location."

Well, what happened after that was crazy.

Four more buildings fell through for a total of six buildings. Yes, six buildings fell through! My sister was getting leery and threatening to go back to the school system. I convinced her we must hang in there. Towards the end, I got discouraged and my sister reminded me of the mission and the pastors were praying for me. I was able to hang in there and believe. My sister and I were each other's back bone and we held on to our faith with everything we had. After months of searching, we finally received a breakthrough.

The seventh building became our building. Yes, the number of completion, seven.

When we finally acquired the building, we thought the worst part was over. Boy were we wrong. The stress in finding the building was minor in comparison to what we experienced after that. The county took us to hell and back to get the building done. There were all kinds of issues and problems with the construction. There were other childcare owners trying to block the opening of our school, calling code enforcement almost every day. We even got a "Stop Work Order" placed on the front door of the building during the process. However, I was now at the point that no matter what happened I would not stop fighting until the doors of our school opened.

Finally, in October 2013, the doors opened and our school, Dream Big, was a reality. It was literally a dream come true. Within the first year of opening, the accolades and blessings were happening. In our first year open, Dream Big was named the Orlando Magic

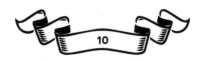

Preschool of the Year. Within fourteen months of opening, we were a million-dollar business. The school was accredited nationally and internationally.

Life looked very different when I started putting my mouth on the things I wanted to see. No, it wasn't easy, but because I was persistent and kept believing, I was able to manifest with my mouth what I wanted.

There is power in your mouth!

My change was intentional because I was tired of living unhappy, unfulfilled, and unsatisfied. I knew something had to change if I was going to keep my sanity. Thank God for the manifestation and change! I'm not who I used to be. I am now who God said I could be!

Because of my struggles, negativity, self-limiting beliefs and scarcity mindset, I stayed stuck for years. Because I don't want anyone to stay stale, stuck, and stagnant like I was, I wrote this book to change lives for the better. This book is particularly for every woman but really for any person who speaks or has spoken negatively about themselves and had negative words spoken to them or over them. I'm here to let you know you don't have to stay stuck in the lie that you've been telling yourself. You don't have to live in the lie people have been telling you. You can change your entire life when you make a right now decision to close your ears to the haters, enemies, frenemies, naysayers, and even your own negative thoughts. Instead, put your mouth on what God says about you.

You have everything within you to walk in your purpose and destiny and go to your next level

Are you ready? Let's go!

PRAYER OF SUCCESS AND NEXT LEVELS

Father God,

Thank You for letting Your perfect will rule and reign in my life as I confess and believe Your perfect plans for my success and next level. I thank You for preparing my heart and my mind to give birth to every promise You put in me. I confess with my mouth that I am elevated to new levels and introduced to new opportunities that I never knew were possible.

Thank You for allowing me to confess what You say and to believe and see what You see. I know that no weapon formed against me shall prosper. Thank You for the strength and tenacity to outlast every challenge, overcome all obstacles, and move past any mountains in my way, so I can have the victory You promised.

Father, because of who You are, I know who I am and Whose I am. I know that I am more than enough. I am more than a conqueror. I am a victor and not a victim of my circumstances. I walk in wealthy places, in the overflow, in the more than enough, in the fullness of your riches and abundance. Success is in every single area of my life, health, relationships, spirit, mind, body, soul, family, wisdom, peace, joy, happiness, divine connections, finances, elevations and

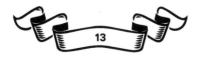

new levels. I confess supernatural breakthroughs, enlargement of my territory, miracles, signs and wonders, and explosive blessings. I thank You for favor surrounding me like a shield, and I also thank You for protection of Your ministering angels.

Thank You for all the lessons and blessings. Thank You for teaching me to use my mouth and put it on Your promises for my life. I magnify and honor You.

These blessings I ask in Your Son, Jesus Christ's name,

Amen

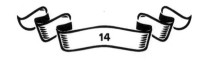

TAME YOUR TONGUE

Your next level—and everything you want out of life—is possible! When you can align your words with God's Word, tame your tongue, put your mouth on what you want to see, and then take the action to make things happen, you can live a limitless life!

Let's discuss why you need to tame your tongue. Our tongue, which is a very small part of our bodies, can be the filthiest, nastiest, most despicable part of our bodies. On the other hand, the tongue can be the best, most magnificent, dream manifesting part of our bodies. Sadly, most people use this part of their mouths to speak negativity and bad things over their situation, life and future. I know, because as I told you earlier, it's what I did for many years. By now, you already know that words have tremendous power and the power of life and death are in the tongue. Knowing this fact, why wouldn't you use your words to help instead of hurt? You have the power and authority to manifest whatever you could possibly want and dream of, if you would just use your words to make it happen!

Let's be honest here— you may go through some trials and tribulations. There is definitely a process. It's not going to fall from the sky into your lap. You've got to put in the work, but yes, it will happen if you do your part, God will definitely do His part. Oh, and guess

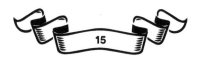

what—here is even better news— when your dream manifests, it will be bigger, better and grander than you could have ever imagined. His ways and thoughts are higher than our thoughts and ways. Knowing these facts, there is no reason for you not to get in alignment with God's Word.

Exciting, right?

But you can't get there until you do one very important thing— tame your tongue.

Have you allowed your tongue to get in the way of your dreams, goals and purpose? Be truthful—have you used the phrases below before?

- **Every time I turn around it's always something.**
- **If it's not one thing it's another.**
- **It happens for everybody but me.**
- **That's impossible.**
- **I'm broke.**
- **I can't afford it.**

The list can go on and on. What I need you to realize is that these tongue-lashing phrases are keeping you stuck. They are keeping you comfortable in your mess. These are the excuses you tell yourself so you can keep settling.

It's time for you to tame your tongue to produce the positive instead of the negative. It's time to produce what you want to see instead of what you don't want to see.

What if you really made a conscious effort to tame your tongue?

What would happen? How could your life change?

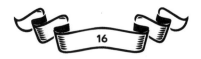

Make a choice to get a **hold of your tongue. It's time to tame it!**

≋ T~ALK~ A~LWAYS~ M~ANIFESTS~ E~NERGY~ ≋

What you talk about is what you give energy to. What you talk about you manifest. The work and energy you put into taming your tongue will be the difference between the life and death of your dreams and next level! You know the saying, "there is power in the tongue." If you learn to tame your tongue, you can stop some of the attacks of the devil. Many times, we stay in trouble because we just can't tame our tongues.

You always have to be right.

You have to *keep it real* You just have to straighten somebody.

You had to get the last word.

You call in mess and then say the devil did it.

No, you did it! You called the devil, opened the door and invited him in! Stop wreaking havoc and chaos because you can't control your tongue. Don't get mad or upset with others because your tongue is controlling you instead of you controlling it.

The good news is you can fix this. Think before you speak. Use your tongue to help and not hurt or get back at people. Slow down, breathe, re-group and tame your tongue to do and say what you want it to say. Tame your tongue so you can see what you want to see and live the life you want to live. Don't allow your tongue to cause you to lose another opportunity, job, relationship or anything else that you want.

The Flip Side

Now, there is a flip side of taming your tongue too. How is that? Well because there are others who won't open their mouth. They watch everyone else realize their dreams and go to their next level, but they are too scared to tame their tongue to ask for what they want. If you don't open your mouth no one can hear you. No one will know what you want if you don't ask. Yep, it's scary if you're used to being quiet, but you have to open your mouth. Be bold if you've never been bold before! It's time! Do it scared!

Practice using your tongue to get what you want.

You could have all the skill and talent in the world and still miss your opportunity because you won't use your tongue to manifest your dream. A closed mouth will never get fed. Open your mouth and put it on what you want to see!

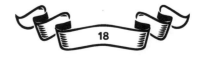

REFLECTIONS

How have you allowed your tongue to block your blessings and dreams?

_____

_____

_____

_____

_____

_____

_____

_____

_____

_____

_____

_____

_____

_____

_____

_____

Think about TAME (Talk Always Manifests Energy). What type of energy are you manifesting when you speak?

_____

_____

_____

_____

_____

_____

_____

_____

_____

_____

_____

_____

_____

_____

_____

_____

_____

_____

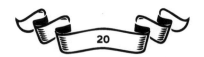

When you speak, are you the energy you want to attract?

_____

_____

_____

_____

_____

_____

_____

_____

_____

_____

_____

_____

_____

_____

_____

_____

_____

_____

WATCH YOUR MOUTH!

Everything we say matters. That is why it's so important for us to be careful about what we say. You must keep your mouth from speaking negativity, especially negative self-talk. Don't ever use your mouth to tear yourself down. You were made in the image of God. That's right, you were fearfully and wonderfully made. When you tear yourself down that's like tearing God down. It's as if you are saying He made a mistake. You may make some mistakes, but God doesn't. He already knew you were going to do that. He knows everything about you and what is going to happen in your life. With that being said, watch your mouth! Keep it from negative self-talk and be easy on yourself.

I know you probably think this topic is nothing to be excited about. You're probably thinking, "I don't need anyone to tell me to watch my mouth."

The truth is—everyone needs a reminder and self-check from time to time.

When life beats you down it can be really hard to stay positive and focused. During these times it can be very easy to miss the mark if you speak in a negative way. Watching your mouth is vital to your purpose, destiny and next level. You can't take back what you say, so

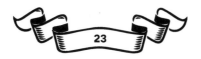

the objective here is to keep your mouth off of anything that will be negative or harmful to someone else or yourself.

As a child you probably heard the saying, "sticks and stones can break my bones, but words can't ever hurt me." I know that you've realized by now that words can hurt people. When people don't watch their mouth, the negative words can have lifelong effects. Negative words have broken up marriages, lost jobs, brought about enemies, hurt feelings, caused conflicts, caused killings and more. Why would you want to be a part of this toxicity? Nope, don't do it!

Negative words serve no purpose or space in your life. Dismiss anything or anyone bringing negativity to you. That is the devil's plan to kill, steal and destroy. Don't allow yourself to take part in the devil's master plan to tear down and destroy hopes and futures.

If the people you are hanging around use their mouth to reflect what you don't want to see in your life, you must reevaluate if you need them in your face. You have to watch all mouths that you are around not just your own because it can definitely make a difference in your life.

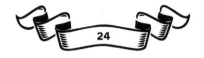

REFLECTIONS

Reflect on a time someone said something negative to you that hurt you. Did it stick with you? How did it make you feel? What positive words could you have spoken over yourself to change how you felt?

_____

_____

_____

_____

_____

_____

_____

_____

_____

_____

_____

_____

_____

_____

_____

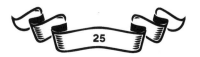

Reflect on a time you used negative self-talk and it made you talk yourself out of doing something to elevate you.

_____

_____

_____

_____

_____

_____

_____

_____

_____

_____

_____

_____

_____

_____

_____

_____

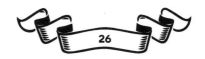

You can't take negative words back, but you can ask God to cancel those words and to forgive you. What words have you spoken over yourself or someone else that you want God to forgive you for and cancel?

_____

_____

_____

_____

_____

_____

_____

_____

_____

_____

_____

_____

_____

_____

_____

_____

_____

You also must forgive yourself and others for negative words spoken over you. Have you forgiven yourself and others for their negative words?

_____

_____

_____

_____

_____

_____

_____

_____

_____

_____

_____

_____

_____

_____

_____

_____

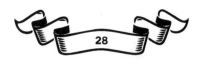

Complaining is another negative area in which you need to watch your mouth. Don't sit and continuously focus on what is wrong in life or what you don't have. What you focus on is what you feed.

Complaining is one of those sins most accepted by Christians. Many times, we tolerate it and perhaps don't even think of it as sin because it happens all the time. The fact that it happens all the time doesn't make it acceptable. Be cognizant of whether you're dealing with a complaint or a concern. Don't allow complaints or complainers to be your norm.

In the Old Testament book of Numbers, the children of Israel constantly complained against Moses, Aaron, and God. We know the enemy doesn't want us to fulfill God's intended purpose for our lives. Complaining is one of the tricks the enemy uses to sneak up on us and distract us. Because it's so easy to complain many of us fall prey to the temptation to gripe, murmur, grumble, and complain, especially when things aren't going our way. Don't do it! This is a sure-fire way to block your blessings.

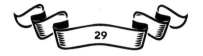

REFLECTIONS

Why is complaining dangerous to you and your purpose and destiny?

_____

_____

_____

_____

_____

_____

_____

_____

_____

_____

_____

_____

_____

_____

_____

_____

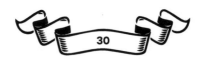

Reflect on an uncomfortable situation you're dealing with now. How can you deal with it without complaining?

_____

_____

_____

_____

_____

_____

_____

_____

_____

_____

_____

_____

_____

_____

_____

_____

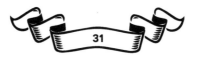

MOUTH TRASH!

Now that we have been reminded to watch our mouths, let's dig deeper.

Do you know what mouth trash is? It's stuff we say with our mouth that needs to be trashed. It's gossiping, judging, cursing and lying. You should never surround yourself with these type of people—run from, block, and delete them from your life.

Your entire destiny can be halted, snatched, and destroyed when you choose to hang around negative, toxic, messy, mean and miserable people who constantly put their mouth on these negative things that don't serve them or you. You can't allow hanging with people with these traits to be your norm. No, I'm not judging anyone. I don't want you to block your blessings hanging around the wrong people that use a bunch of mouth trash and who have the wrong mindset. You shouldn't want this for yourself either. Guard yourself from the wrong people.

I know what you are thinking—"What if it's a family member?"

We all have them! It's unfortunate, but we can't choose our family. However, we can choose what we allow, and what you allow will continue—good or bad. You don't have to allow anyone to

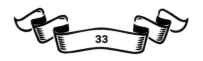

trap you in their mouth trash, even family members. You have a couple of choices. You can address it and see if it gets better. You may have to love that family member from afar until things change or, worst case scenario, you may have to cut them off all together. Don't allow anyone to entrap you and cause you to lose out on the promises of God.

After you have cleaned up the mouth trash around you, make sure to clean up yourself too. It happens to everyone from time to time. Good thing for us our God is a forgiving God. If you do slip up (which we know happens sometimes), get back on track immediately.

Clean Up The Lies

We must touch on lying because it is a huge part of mouth trash that can stop your destiny. Every person on the planet has told an Oscar-winning lie in their life. Haven't we all lied without being caught? When we can do it and get away with it then it's easy to continue to do. We know "thou shalt not lie" is one of the Ten Commandments, yet most of us fall short. With this being said, I believe most of us know putting our mouth on lies will not get us anywhere, In fact, lies will only hold us back. However, we need to talk about lies because you want to make sure you are not attached to liars and that you are not one yourself.

The Bible has several scriptures on lying to let you know the consequences that comes with lies.

Do not let any unwholesome talk come out of your mouths,
but only what is helpful for building others up according to their needs,
that it may benefit those who listen.
•• Ephesians 4:29 ••

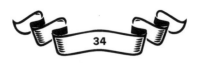

The lip of truth shall be established for ever:
but a lying tongue is but for a moment.
•• Proverbs 12:19 ••

Why do we lie? Many times, we have a problem with the truth and the fact that it doesn't always serve our purposes. If you think like I used to think, it makes us feel better or keeps us out of trouble. When you can take the made-up route of your imagination, it allows you to run from your fears and your truth.

Do you know that the biggest lies told are the ones we tell ourselves?

Because of past mistakes you may feel hopeless or doomed, so you choose to lie to yourself and then eventually you have to lie to others to cover up your truth. I'm not talking about those white lies here, that's not the focus. It's those lies that are stealing your destiny and joy. Those lies we allow other people to feed us or that we feed to ourselves that cause us to be stifled into a life of mediocrity and blame.

Lies and liars can destroy lives! You're not who they say you are so stop telling yourself that lie! You are who God says you are so put your mouth and thoughts on that. It's time to hit the "Refresh" button and start again.

It's your time win! It's time for new levels! You will begin to win and truly live a life of purpose by telling yourself the truth. Tell yourself the truth in your, in everything you do... your thinking, your personal and professional relationships, your career or business, and the most important relationship—the one you have with yourself.

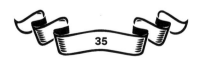

This is where the biggest, most dangerous lies are told. Make that shift and decide to walk in your own truth. Start telling the truth. Level-up and get rid of the lies and the mess.

Honesty is paramount, and it's always where you need to begin, for your success, happiness and self-esteem. It's not fun to be reminded of the humbling fact that we shouldn't lie, but everyone needs to be regularly reminded to be truthful in our speaking and in our hearts. All of us are susceptible to lying from time to time. We all know what it's like to take comfort in the escape, but I still want to remind you to use your mouth to speak truth. This will help you to ensure your actions are aligning with your words.

Clean Up Cursing

Cursing is some serious mouth trash! When we feel angry, upset, impatient, frustrated or stuck in situations that we can't control it can be difficult to edit the words heading from our brain to our tongue at the speed of lightning. Before we know it, we have put our mouth on something we shouldn't have. But the words that emerge from our mouth can have a real and lasting impact. Keep your mouth clean.

Clean up the cursing. I know it's not easy, especially when it's a habit. I've had to work on this myself too. Sometimes you can do really well and not curse and then one thing happens that sets you off and your mouth starts to take control. I've been there many times. I had to make a conscious effort to control my mouth and you will too if this has been an issue for you. If you mess up don't stay there recognize the issue and fix it!

Remember, you can't take back what you say. Also, it is necessary to note, cursing doesn't just involve profanity.

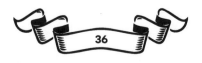

Some people use their mouths to dispel curses on people. The Bible talks about it. Witchcraft and sorcery exists, but it's not something you should put your mouth on or deal with as a believer of Christ.

Clean Up Judging

Judging is another form of mouth trash. This is one of those things, like complaining, that many Christians accept as okay and don't realize it's sinful. You don't want to be judged and it's certainly not your place to judge others. Don't use your mouth to make judgements against others that God didn't make. Don't judge a book by its cover. You are out of your territory and league. The Bible has many scriptures about judging others. It's best to refrain and leave the judgement to God.

"Judge not, that you be not judged. For with the judgment you pronounce you will be judged, and with the measure you use it will be measured to you. Why do you see the speck that is in your brother's eye, but do not notice the log that is in your own eye? Or how can you say to your brother, 'Let me take the speck out of your eye,' when there is the log in your own eye? You hypocrite, first take the log out of your own eye, and then you will see clearly to take the speck out of your brother's eye.

•• Matthew 7:1-5 ••

Clean Up The Gossiping

Gossiping is such a negative trait. This is one of the worst types of mouth trash there is. Gossip is defined as: "information about the behavior or personal life of other people, often without the full truth being revealed or known."

Gossip can also be information about a person or behavior that is spread intentionally in an effort to shame, embarrass, slander and ruin the person's reputation. Gossiping many times involves negativity, complaining, lying and judging of people. Anyone who has been living long enough has experienced the harmful and hurtful effects of gossip before. Even if the person talking didn't mean direct harm, the result of gossip is betrayal or broken trust, anger, hurt feelings and other negative effects. The Bible clearly warns us to stay away from those people who gossip and to guard our words when we speak about others! Keep your mouth clear of gossip. Don't start it and don't feed into it. We can get caught up in in a cycle of drama and confusion so easy just by listening to someone gossiping so don't only guard your mouth against gossip also make sure you guard your ears too.

REFLECTIONS

Now that we know and understand mouth trash and can fully walk in our truth, lets reflect on the following:

What is your truth about where you are right now in life? Are you where you want to be?

_____

_____

_____

_____

_____

_____

_____

_____

_____

_____

_____

_____

_____

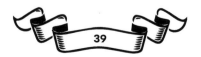

Are you happy with your truth? If not, how can you fix it? If yes, what can you do to take it to the next level? What words can you use to take you where you want to go?

_____

_____

_____

_____

_____

_____

_____

_____

_____

_____

_____

_____

_____

_____

_____

_____

_____

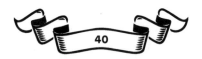

We can't choose our family members, but we can make decisions or choices that will allow us to live and walk in peace. How do you deal with a family member or friend who is toxic and constantly dwelling in mouth trash?

_____

_____

_____

_____

_____

_____

_____

_____

_____

_____

_____

_____

_____

_____

_____

_____

_____

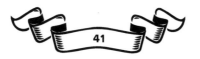

TRIBING AND VIBING

Watching your mouth is much easier to do when you surround yourself with people who are doing the same thing. Surround yourself with quality people. You need people that can elevate you and push you, not ones that feed into disorder and chaos. Your next level journey will take you through several ups and downs. Life will take you through some things that you never expected good and bad. As this happens you need people who are going to support you and uplift you through those times. You also will need people who will tell you the truth and be real with you, not sugar coat stuff to make you feel good. Feeling good has never taught any lessons.

I love the phrase, "Your Vibe Attracts Your Tribe." I believe this to be one hundred percent true. Your true and real tribe gets you. They, for the most part, understand you and accept you as you are. You can be your true authentic self with your tribe.

As you start to evolve and begin to put your mouth on the things you really want, your current tribe may end up changing. This is what happened to me. As I said in the beginning of this book, I was very negative. My energy and vibes were low. Negativity was the norm. Everything I was putting out I was getting back. My friends and I were just alike. No, they weren't bad people and I wasn't a bad person

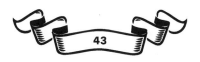

either, but we all had bad energy.

Watch the energy of your tribe. The wrong energy will kill your dreams and destiny. If they have bad energy, low energy, slow energy, or no energy, a procrastination spirit, or are full of excuses, their energy can rub off on you. I was a science teacher so I'm going to give a little example here to bring home my point.

An ion is an atom or group of atoms that carry a positive or negative electric charge. If you have more negative (electrons) than positive (protons) guess what happens—the charge becomes negative. If you have more protons (positive) than electrons (negative) the ion becomes positive.

It's the same with people. If you have more negative in your life than positive, then that's what you will get out of life. The opposite is also true—if you have more positive than negative you will get positive out of life. The bottom line here is, if you choose to hang around people with low energy, bad habits, and bad vibes, the odds are you won't be able to break those things off of you.

You may be thinking to yourself, "I can change them." Don't get caught in that trap. If you were already in a bad space and now you have a brand new perspective that you're going to change, your change isn't going to come hanging around the same people that kept you down. It's just like saying, "Oh, just because they smoke doesn't mean I'm going to smoke." If you hang around people who smoke all the time you will be affected, even if you don't smoke yourself. You will smell like smoke. You will still inhale the toxic fumes. How many people have died from second hand smoke?

The day I made up my mind to change my life and decided that I was going to go after my next level, I was so excited. I started to talk

to the people in my circle, but things didn't go like I thought. As I talked about my dreams and changing my life, they didn't seem to be excited. In fact, they felt like I was leaving them behind. There was judgement and things didn't feel comfortable in this tribe anymore. Family, friends, and co-workers didn't get it. I don't know why I thought they would feel what I was feeling. Just because I changed didn't mean they were going to change. The vibe was changing, and I started moving away from my familiar into something new. As I moved away with a new attitude and a positive vibe, the new tribe I was coming into seemed to have the same vibe. It was the positive energy I needed in my life. No, I didn't just drop all of my former friends and I couldn't do away with my family, but I spent less and less time with them and we eventually grew apart.

As you start to come into your new place of freedom you will experience the pains of letting go. Sometimes we outgrow people and that's okay. You have to go on the path that is right for you. As time goes on the old and new tribe can co-mingle if the ones in the old tribe level up but if not, that is okay. You just need to move on in a new direction.

In the beginning of your new walk your circle may even fluctuate. You will see the energy change and some in your circle may pull you up and others you may pull up. It's nothing wrong with helping but don't let your helping others pull you down. Keep your energy high. Keeping your energy and your circle high will keep you focused on the right things. As you do this your talk will continue to move to more of what you do want and not what you don't want. Vibrate higher!

Motivational speaker Jim Rohn said, "You are the average of the five people you spend the most time with." Believe it or not, we are influenced most by those closest to us and who are we are spending

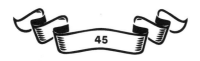

the most time with. There was a study at Harvard University that showed the people we speak with and hang around on a regular basis determines up to 95 percent of our failure or success. With this statistic, it is vital that we have the right tribe and they are speaking our language.

The people we engage in conversation with on a regular basis definitely play a role in our thoughts, actions, words and deeds. We get advice from these people. We are seeing their lifestyles. We usually know their every move and they usually know ours. What is your tribe talking about? What is coming from their mouth? How is their energy?

We must pay attention to our circle. Your goal should be to make sure your tribe is the vibe you want to be around. Choose to be around like-minded people with even bigger goals than yours. Get around people that inspire you and uplift you. Make sure your tribe is pushing you to aim higher, dream bigger, go harder and put your mouth on things that will take you to greater levels. Yes, you need your own VIP club that's on fire for the best things in life. The ones that are in search of greatness and purpose. Mediocrity and average should not be a part of the tribe you subscribe to. Why deal with average or even good when you can have great? Put your mouth on it!

When you decide to put your mouth on the higher things in life and move to greatness, your tribe has got to be on point. The bar has got to be set high. Your tribe should be stretching you to vibrate high and only put your mouth on things that will grow you and increase you.

Goal getters, early risers, burning the midnight oil, grinding and pushing to see their dreams that is the circle you must seek if you want to see your purpose and destiny fulfilled.

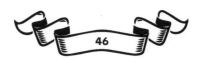

REFLECTIONS

Your Ideal Tribe

Use this page to describe what your ideal tribe should look like to you. Be very detailed about what you want in your tribe.

_____

_____

_____

_____

_____

_____

_____

_____

_____

_____

_____

_____

_____

_____

_____

_____

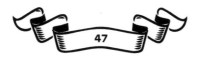

Tribe Thoughts

Who are the people in your Top 5?

1. _____

2. _____

3. _____

4. _____

5. _____

How do these people show up in your life? What do they bring to the table?

1. _____

2. _____

3. _____

4. _____

5. _____

Do they look like the circle you described?

1. _____

2. _____

3. _____

4. _____

5. _____

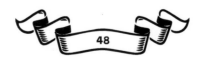

Are they a help or hindrance?

1. _____

2. _____

3. _____

4. _____

5. _____

Do they have high or low energy?

1. _____

2. _____

3. _____

4. _____

5. _____

How do you support them?

1. _____

2. _____

3. _____

4. _____

5. _____

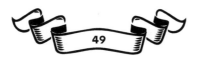

How do they support you?

1. _____

2. _____

3. _____

4. _____

5. _____

Think hard dig deep. Is your tribe really your vibe?

_____

_____

_____

_____

_____

_____

_____

_____

_____

_____

_____

_____

_____

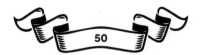

THE WORD

Our words are so crucial to our success or failure and next level. As I write this book, I remember when and where God gave me this title. I already knew I was going to write a book about purpose, success, and winning. I already knew my story could help someone. It was the solution to someone's problem. I understood what happened to, and for, me, and I was meant to share it.

Here was the issue—I simply had no clue on what to title it. I was on a plane on my way to Las Vegas thinking about my life and how it had drastically changed. I was sitting in first class—something I used to think I could never afford. I thought about why my life had changed. What was the catalyst for the major change? In that moment, I realized it was my words!

I always believed in God. I went to church and in general I thought of myself as a good, nice Christian woman. However, the essential problem with me was the words I used and the words the people around me were using.

My words kept me stuck. They caused me doubt and made me question my faith all the time. I realized I was just existing in the world before instead of living. Wow! I didn't even realize I was existing but now I do! Now I know I'm living! It was not until I changed my

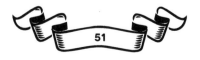

words and aligned them with God's word that I became unstuck, moved past doubt, started having crazy ridiculous faith and began to really start living! Right there on that plane God gave me the title for this book! At that moment, I had a revelation that my words made all the difference in the world.

God hears every word we say. God also carefully examines every single word that comes from our mouths. Now that's deep! There is not a word that touches your tongue that God doesn't hear. When you really think about it words control everything.

Do you realize that words are so important to God that He actually said, I am the Word, the Truth, and the Light?" God uses His Word to rule life. In the same way, we use our words to rule our lives. This is why you can't take the words you use lightly!

We hear it all the time and it sounds cliché that there is life and death in the power of the tongue. It's not cliché though, it is the truth! The words that come from our mouth really do create our reality. This is why the things that you put your mouth on are so vital to your life and success.

Do you really know what it means to put your mouth on something? To put your mouth on something is the same as holding hands with someone and touching and agreeing. When you put your mouth on something, it's put into the atmosphere. It is getting in agreement. It is an alignment.

When you say the wrong words, you mess up your alignment. This will slow down or all together stop your assignment. We are here for a divine purpose and assignment. Don't mess it up and steal your own destiny.

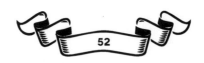

The question though is who are you getting in agreement with?

Who are you aligning with?

Many times, we open our mouth and align with the devil. We align with things and people we really should not be aligned with. When we open our mouths, we are planting whether we realize it or not. What are you planting when you speak?

Words are seeds that are planted!
Words are seeds that connect!
Words are seeds that breed!
Words are seeds that bring harvest!
Words are seeds that bring opportunities!
Words are seeds that bring change!

We have to fix our words to be what we want to see. We have to say the words that God would want us to say. As we think about words being seeds and how seeds scatter, it should change our thoughts on how we use our words. Think before you speak! Words really do matter!

Research has shown that the average person has about 12,000 to 60,000 thoughts per day. Of those thoughts, can you guess what percentage of them are negative? A staggering 80% of a person's thoughts are negative. This is on a daily basis. Out of your 12,000 to 60,000 thoughts per day, 95 percent of those thoughts are the same repetitive thoughts as the day before and 80% of those are negative just like the day before. As you think these negative thoughts, they end up coming out of your mouth as negative words.

We have far more words in our vocabulary that express negative thoughts and emotions rather than positive emotions so it's no

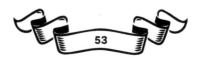

surprise that there is so much negativity spoken! It's easy to speak negatively because most people do it! But you don't have to be in the most people category. In the word of Les Brown, " we must do what others won't so we can have what they don't!" We don't have to be like most and use negative words all the time. Make the decision to do something different.

Those that are looking to live, walk, and achieve a life of purpose and destiny must choose words that are positive and uplifting.

If you think about instances in your life when people have used words that were mean, nasty and negative when they spoke to you and how it made you feel, why would you just shoot words out of your mouth? Words influence others. Words build relationships. Words impact lives. Words make conversations. Words can be potent! Words can be magical! Words hurt or words can help. Words basically make the world go round. Words control the world!

One word can change everything! As you can see words really do make an impact and they are critical to your life. Think about the quotes in the world, what are they? They are words! Words are vital to each and every life!

My advice—Choose your words wisely! Put your mouth on things that will serve you and show you what you want to see!

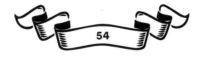

REFLECTIONS

Do you think before you speak? Why is this important to your success?

_____

_____

_____

_____

_____

_____

_____

_____

_____

_____

_____

_____

_____

_____

_____

_____

_____

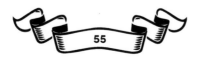

Do the words you use every day define who you are and what you are about?

_____

_____

_____

_____

_____

_____

_____

_____

_____

_____

_____

_____

_____

_____

_____

_____

_____

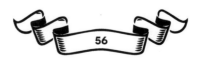

Do you use words to help people or cut them down?

_____

_____

_____

_____

_____

_____

_____

_____

_____

_____

_____

_____

_____

_____

_____

_____

_____

_____

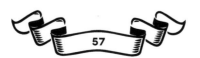

Do your words show your intelligence or ignorance?

_____

_____

_____

_____

_____

_____

_____

_____

_____

_____

_____

_____

_____

_____

_____

_____

_____

_____

_____

_____

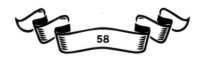

SEED AND HARVEST TIME

We learned in the last chapter that when you open your mouth and let out words you are planting seeds. What you plant is what you will harvest. When you speak words, you bring them into the atmosphere and give them life. You are prophesying your future with your words.

In Genesis 8:22, it is promised while the Earth remains seed and harvest time will not cease. As long as you are opening your mouth and using your words as the Bible said—seed and harvest time will not cease.

When we sow we want to sow good gifts. We want to sow gifts from our hearts and gifts that are pleasing to God. Think about it. Are your words pleasing to God? Are you truly sowing seeds of joy and happiness? What about peace and goodness? Can you honestly answer yes to these questions?

If you are not sowing good, then you are obviously putting your mouth on that which is bad. Do you sow discord and negativity and then wonder why things are chaotic and crazy in your life?

I remember some years ago before I was really watching my words and putting my mouth on the things I wanted to see, I was

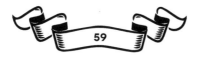

scrolling through Facebook and started commenting on a picture I saw. I said to the person with me, "Ooh child, she looks a hot mess, old and tore down. She should have never posted that picture."

The person with me said, "You know she is sick, right?"

I was quick to say, "She sure looks it too."

What a mess that I would think that and then open my mouth to say something so negative. I was sowing mean seeds and negativity. As I was sowing and putting my mouth on foolishness, guess what—I was also reaping a harvest of the same thing, but it never dawned on me at the time. After all, I grew up around a bunch of gossip and tearing people down. Praise God, I know better and now do better. I'm about goals instead of gossip. I can't deal with people who do this anymore. I'm glad God is forgiving because I needed plenty of it in those days and I know I wasn't by myself and for this reason I want to help as many people as I can, particularly women.

You probably already know, and statistics show, women gossip much more than men. Since women are the ones who gossip the most, I want to challenge every woman who is reading this book to put their mouth on better outcomes. When you plant lemon seeds, you get lemons not apples or oranges. It's the same thing with your mouth. What you plant is what you harvest! If you are looking for a big harvest you need to plant plenty of good seeds.

Are you getting it yet? You must plant what you want to see. That means say what it is you want to see even if you don't see it. This is a very simple principle that is very hard to conceive for many people. I need to throw in another good scripture here and it's Proverbs 6:22 which says—You are snared by the words of your mouth. This means you are trapped by the words of your mouth. What you think may

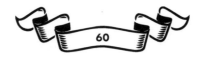

not trap you, but your words surely will. Once the words are put into the atmosphere you change the whole game! You must watch what you say. When it's in your head that's one thing. When you let it out of your head you take it to a whole new level.

So many times, people get close to their dreams and then they kill everything they worked for with their mouth. Why would you work so hard and throw it all away at the end? If there is one thing I want you to get, it is the fact that you must be intentional with what you put your mouth on. This is what many of us do, we run the race and when we near the finish line and something unplanned happens, we use our mouth to say something like this— "Oh well, I knew it wasn't going to happen anyway."

This is like running a football 99 yards down the field and then dropping the ball on the 1-yard line. At this point you have two options. You could let the mistake haunt you and ruin the way you play the rest of the game or you can stay in the game and make a touchdown on the next play. If there is still time on the clock, you have a chance to win. Unplanned things will happen in life, but we don't need to plant seeds of negativity when plans fall through. We don't need to kill everything we did to work towards our vision or dream because of a mishap. The mishaps, the mistakes, the issues build character and are preparation for the dream and vision.

Words are real! Seed and harvest time is also real! If we don't give up, we will see the harvest! If you plant God's words and His will, you will not falter or fail. Use your words to plant so many good seeds you can't keep count and believe your harvest will come back to you. When I say plant so many seeds I mean for you to do just that. I want you to get aggressive about your next level, your dreams, goals, and vision.

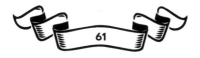

When we get aggressive with our seed sowing in order to reap the harvest, we can't just be sowers, we must be movers. In order to see the seeds grow, I know that you know you must water the seeds that have been planted. You may need to fertilize and nurture the planted seeds.

In other words, "Do the work!"

Dreams work when you do. Cultivate your dreams! Take action and make sure you do your part to help your seeds grow.

In life watering our seeds is where faith comes in. Faith, as we know, is the substance of things hoped for and the evidence of things not seen. When we plant our words in hope, we have got to stand on God's word so we can see the evidence of what we say. This is what it means to take care of our seeds. When we plant seeds during the nurturing phase it may take a while to see the harvest. While waiting on the harvest you must stand in faith and not give up. I know waiting is the hardest part of the process, but you have to go through the process.

The process is necessary and not optional. Your process is different and unique to your situation. You can't follow what someone else went through but you must go through your own process.

During the process is the part the devil will really work hard to sneak his way into your space to steal, kill, and destroy. You may not see anything in the natural during this time, but you must see it in the spirit and continue to keep your mouth on the seeds planted. While waiting for your harvest this is where you draw closer to God. Stay in prayer during seed and harvest time. Expect the unexpected and speak what you want to see!

REFLECTIONS

Reflect on a time you have allowed your words to snare you. What lesson did you learn from doing that?

_____

_____

_____

_____

_____

_____

_____

_____

_____

_____

_____

_____

_____

_____

_____

_____

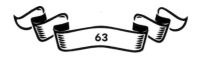

THE NEXT LEVEL CHALLENGE

Now that you have read this book, it is my hope and belief that you have made the decision to go to your next level and put your mouth on the things you want to see happen in your life. Yes, you have read the book, but I know you know there is more to do. It's time to do the work!

WARNING!

This is the part where most people who are longing to reach their dreams fall off. People will read, research, interview others, write, and take classes, but when it comes to the execution, many people just aren't willing to stick it out and execute with everything they have.

What about you?

Are you ready to change your life by planning for your next level?

Are you really ready to move forward to achieve your goals, walk in your purpose, and emerge to your destiny?

It's time for your NEXT LEVEL!

If you are really ready, now it's time for you to go on a journey

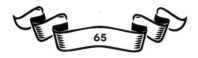

to discover your true authentic self and really uncover everything about you and what you need to do to breakthrough barriers, to become unstuck and go to your next level. All of the steps are important to achieving success! Be ready use your mouth to win in all you do. Put your mouth on all the things you want to see!

Make The Commitment

It's your time to commit to your commitments. It's time for you to stretch yourself! It's time for you to push harder than you've ever pushed before! It's time to get ignited about your life! After all, you only have one. There are no do-overs and there is no time to waste!

Now is YOUR TIME to:

- Act!
- Set the tone for your NEXT LEVEL!
- Set and stick to your goals
- Put your mouth on what you want to see
- Stay focused
- Be Intentional

Claim and see your Next Level

While this is not going to be too time-consuming, it is going to involve work. Some days will require more work than others. I am going to ask you to consider your goals and question yourself on everything! In order to slay in life, you must first take an inside look at yourself.

Another WARNING!

Get ready to see some major changes! You are not going to believe how easy it is to live a successful life when you decide to be

intentional, apply these simple steps, and always use your mouth to say what you want to see. As you complete your work please make sure you have the following:

- Open Mind
- Determination
- Honesty
- Journal
- Pens
- Markers
- Glue Sticks
- Magazines/Pictures

YOUR IDEAL DAY

If you can see the invisible, speak what seems to be the impossible, and believe it, you most certainly can achieve it!

Use this space to write out what an ideal day would look like for you. Think BIG! Dream BIG! There are no limits or boundaries as to how your ideal day should look like from start to finish. Be very detailed and specific.

_____

_____

_____

_____

_____

_____

_____

_____

_____

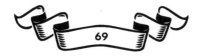

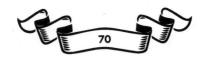

ESTABLISH A MORNING ROUTINE

One of the most important ways to prepare for your next level of success is to establish a morning routine. Do you have a morning routine? If not, it's time to get one! If you do have one it may need to be tweaked.

Morning routines are essential. Be mindful of how you start your day and what you say when you wake up every morning. Below is a list of the six things successful people do in the morning. You may not do every single one of these things but a few of these should be in your morning routine. Your routine needs to be specific to you and you need to make it a ritual. Consistency is key!

1. Take the first waking minutes of the day to pray and give God thanks.
2. Meditate silently and write down what you hear every day.
3. Read something inspirational, motivational, or something that will grow you.
4. Journal.
5. Affirmations.
6. Exercise.

Write out a morning routine for yourself in the space below.

_____

_____

_____

_____

_____

_____

_____

_____

_____

_____

_____

_____

_____

_____

_____

_____

_____

_____

_____

YOU AREN'T YOUR MISTAKES

Many of us have greatness within us but we are so overwhelmed with life. When we can't figure out how to get everything done, we get stuck. Guess what happens when we get stuck. We start to say and think the wrong things. We put our mouth on things that cause us to remain stuck.

In our stuckness (a word I made up), we kill our dreams and many of the things God has planned for us. I know there have been issues that have weighed you down in life and ones that may still be weighing you down—failed relationships, financial setbacks, job dissatisfaction and so much more. On top of all of the issues, we magnify the situation when we put our mouth on negative things. I challenge you today to do something different!

I have struggled with this too!

We stay stuck in our mistakes and failures too long. We know we've made mistakes, but we aren't our mistakes and failures. Those are situations that happened for you, not to you. Mistakes don't define you or determine your destiny. We can't conquer what we can't face! Today, choose to face all mistakes and failures.

Remember, you aren't your mistakes or failures!

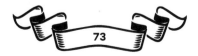

Success solidifies your ability to win and makes your ego feel good, but mistakes and failures teach you valuable lessons. Though we don't like this part of the journey, it is so necessary!

List 5 of the biggest mistakes or failures you have made in life and what you learned from them.

_____

_____

_____

_____

_____

_____

_____

_____

_____

_____

_____

_____

_____

_____

_____

_____

_____

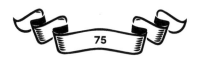

TIME TO LET GO

Today, I _____ choose to let go of any mistakes or failures.

I've experienced and move forward. I know I was created by the Great I AM.

I commit to my greatness!

I have a purpose and destiny and it will be fulfilled.

Today, I choose to put my mouth on what God says I can have and not what I see in the natural.

I am necessary and essential to the world and I make a difference.

I'm letting go of the old and walking into the new!

To My Success and Next Level.

_____

Your Signature Here

NEXT LEVEL YOUR DAY

Can you take one hour to work towards your NEXT LEVEL? One hour a day to change your life!

Aren't you worth it? Don't you deserve it?

You must take time for you during this challenge. I'm asking that you devote at least one hour to yourself every day to whatever you need to do to work on your dreams. If you have more time, that's even better.

Success doesn't happen overnight. Sometimes when you see people you may think that their life just happened...NOT! I bet if you talk to anyone who has really found success you will find out that it was a process that took time and work.

Take time to pray, meditate, and do the activities. Celebrate your wins during this challenge and make a big deal of this because this is the start of the new you and new life you are putting your mouth on and creating for yourself.

You must be serious. Keep your mind and mouth on what you want to see. Don't take it lightly! You'll want to find a quiet space

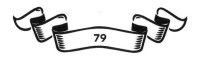

where you won't be disturbed and where you can really focus on what you need to do. You will get out what you put in! As you put in the time each day will get better. This is how you NEXT LEVEL your day and your life.

One day at a time… one step at a time.

It will be better if you are consistent with the time you choose. It's a part of establishing your routine and getting your groove. As we know, life happens so it may be a day you will have to switch times and that's okay but push to really be consistent. Are you ready…Get Set….Let's Go!

Be the change you want to see!

Change is one of those things people don't really like to think about or be a part of. If you want to ever reach your ultimate success, change is a major part of that process so you might as well make up your mind to just embrace it.

I know thoughts, habits and patterns are hard to break, and it actually gets harder as you grow older. It's not surprising that many people have struggled to sustain long-term changes in their behavior and life. If you can understand there is a strong correlation between your thinking and your actions, you will have more power to stay focused on your objectives and therefore it's more likely that you will attain the goals you set.

Do you feel me? Glad you do.

Here are seven steps to make your change more structured and bearable!

7 Steps to Make Change Easier

1. Identify what changes need to be made and make up your mind to do it.

2. Set goals for your change (long term, short term, now goals)

3. Schedule or plan each step

4. Make the change non-negotiable

5. Monitor your progress

6. Address issues and correct

7. Acknowledge progress and success

Change does not happen overnight. It's a one step, one day at a time continuous process. Most people give up because they look for instant gratification. If that's you that means you have some growing to do. Stay the course, remember why you started this process and keep pushing. Remember, this change is non-negotiable! Put your mouth on it and work to make it happen!

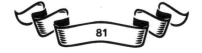

What change(s) do you want to see in your life in the next 30 days? Be very specific. I have allotted extra pages for you to list all of the changes you want to see; you can include why this change is necessary and the necessary steps to make the change happen.

_____

_____

_____

_____

_____

_____

_____

_____

_____

_____

_____

_____

_____

_____

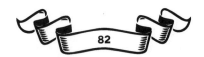

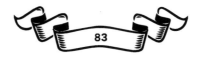

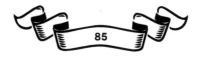

WRITE THE VISION!

In this section, you are going to create your vision pages. These pages should include pictures pertaining to your goals and where you are going in life.

How to Create a Vision Pages:

STEP ONE:

Gather the supplies you need: glue sticks, magazines, pictures, and scissors.

STEP TWO:

During this time, focus on what you really want. Focus and set your intentions on crushing your goals! This will help sum up what your vision pages are about and will also help direct your choice of pictures and words to build your collage around. Make sure to add some good music while creating your pages. Have fun as you create and frame your future! Put your mouth on it as you're doing it. Know why you're placing each picture, word, or phrase on your pages.

STEP THREE:

Cut out pictures, words and phrases to create your vision pages. Now it's time to find the pictures, words and phrases that illustrate your mental image. Look in magazines, brochures, catalogs and

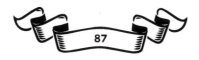

advertisements for pictures, or you can take new photos or use ones you already have.

STEP FOUR:

Meditate on your vision pages. Vision boards are powerful and now you have vision pages that you can look at every day and what's even better about vision pages they are in this book so are handy and you can not only look at them every day but you can carry them with you everywhere you go! You can grab this book and look at your pages when you wake up or when you got to bed. This is invaluble! Spend time daily looking at the pictures and thinking about how you will feel when you will feel when you have completed tasks illustrated on your pages.

The pictures you have pasted on your vision pages provide you with a visual target for your goals. Make a practice of meditating on your vision pages regularly. Take some quiet time to look at and absorb the pictures you placed on your pages. Each picture, word or phrase reflects your passions, interests and desires that you will manifest.

Don't rush this process. Be very intentional. These pages you create will have power and they will work in manifesting your dreams! Be intentional!!!

Lastly, you must put your visualization into action. You must take steps toward the dreams you have put on your pages. For example, if you have posted pictures of your dream vacation, act by purchasing a book about that destination. If you want a million-dollar home, go take a tour of houses in the neighborhood you want to live in. Whatever it is, do something. When you do your part, by putting your mouth on what you want to see and then act, you will powerfully attract your dreams to you like a magnet and speed up your manifestation.

MY VISION

[paste your images here]

MY VISION

[paste your images here]

MY VISION

[paste your images here]

MY VISION

[paste your images here]

MY VISION

[paste your images here]

MY VISION

[paste your images here]

MY VISION

[paste your images here]

MY VISION

[paste your images here]

MY VISION

[paste your images here]

AFFIRM YOURSELF

During the process of making a change in your life and manifesting your next level you will need to implement the power of positive affirmations. An affirmation is a short simple statement that has a huge amount of power.

Create a minimum of 5 positive affirmations of things you want to see happen. The affirmations you are creating are affirming what you want to see happen for you. Make sure your affirmations also align with the vision pages you created. Write the affirmations as if your vision has already come to pass. Speak things that are not as though they were (Romans 4:17). Put your mouth on your next level and what you want to see.

Affirmation Examples:
I am a world-famous singer. I am a money magnet.
Use the space below to write your own affirmations

1. _____

2. _____

3. _____

4. _____

5. _____

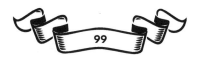

Now begin to say verbal affirmations about your vision pages daily. Say words out loud to yourself daily, and soon they will become ingrained in you and a permanent part of your thinking. Believe that your affirmations will come to pass and watch it work!

AFFORMATIONS

Afformations take affirmations a step further and dig deeper into the statement by asking questions. This concept was founded by Noah St. John, author of "The Secret Code of Success."

St. John believed that the subconscious mind had a better response to questions rather than conscious statements. The questions you ask need to be empowering. These questions will answer the why of your affirmation statement.

Afformation Examples:

Why am I a world-famous singer

Why am I a money magnet?

1. _____

2. _____

3. _____

4. _____

5. _____

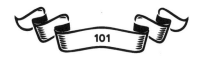

Do you see the difference?

When you answer the affirmation, it affirms the why for your affirmation. Now, go ahead and write five afformations for the affirmations you have written and also answer the afformations. You will use your afformations when you start to questions yourself on whether or not you are good enough or whether or not you can really make it. When you feel doubtful about your dreams, goals, and visions just pull out your afformations and get pumped up!

STAYING CONSISTENT BEYOND
THE CHALLENGE

We are
what we repeatedly do.
EXCELLENCE,
then, is not an act,
but a habit.

• Aristotle •

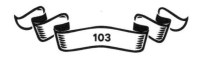

ABOUT THE AUTHOR

Rynette Upson-Bush, aka "The Purpose Pusher", is a power house speaker, certified educator, motivation mentor, and emcee. Her passion and adoration for helping people has moved her to chase her life's calling to educate, empower and enlighten people, particularly women, on how to see more wealth, success, and happiness in life. Rynette has helped hundreds of youth and women find their purpose and calling through her gifts of speaking, motivation and empowerment.

Rynette has spoken for schools, youth empowerment seminars, church groups, women's conferences and correctional institutes. She co-authored two fictional books and is the author of the "Spark Your Life Spark Your Vision Journal" and her latest book, Put Your Mouth On It.

Rynette's mission is to put her unique footprints in the sand and impact the world to reach for their NEXT LEVEL. She wants to empower as many people as she can to put their mouth on their dreams.

She says, "Life wasn't always as it is now. Living in a negative world made me doubt and question who I was and why I even existed. I never felt like I was enough or worthy of anything more than what life handed me but when I got around the right people my whole world changed! I have learned the power of my words

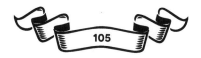

and that I can put my mouth on my dreams and manifest what God says I can have!!! When I learned to do this, I started living instead of existing. I'm now in alignment with my God given assignment and walking in purpose and destiny. You can do this too when you put your mouth on what you want."

Rynette is married with a blended family of seven children and resides in Orlando, Florida. She enjoys spending time with her family and traveling around the world spreading her powerful message to put your mouth on your dreams.

AFTER THOUGHTS

Congratulate yourself! You did it! Only 20 to 40 percent of people actually finish books that they start. I gather that you are serious about putting your mouth on your dreams and next level. You are on your way!

What were your top five takeaways?

1. _____

2. _____

3. _____

4. _____

5. _____

WHAT'S NEXT

So what is your next? What steps will you take to move towards your dream? Get some deadlines on it and make it happen!

Write out your steps below.

_____

_____

_____

_____

_____

_____

_____

_____

_____

_____

_____

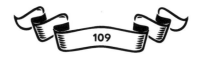

STAY CONNECTED

Did you enjoy the book? Let me know!

You can do this by:

1. Take a selfie of you with the book and
    tag me @rynetteupsonbush on FB and @
    nextlevelchickscollaborate on IG

2. When you do your post tell everyone your top 2
    takeaways from the book. Then tell them to get
    their copy.

3. Leave an Amazon review even if you didn't buy
    it on Amazon.

IG@nextlevelchicks.com   FB @rynetteupsonbush

Linked In@Rynette Upson   Twitter@Rynette Upson

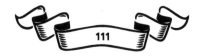

Rynette Upson Bush

TABLE OF GREATNESS

★ 1 DAY LIVE EVENT ★

that gives you the blue print steps to your greatness so you can not just demand your seat at the table but build your own table.

Step Into Your Next Level of Greatness

WWW.RYNETTESPEAKS.COM

— *Master Workshops & Seminars* —
Adults, Youth, Corporate

Women's Motivation and Empowerment · Entrepreneurship · Youth Empowerment
Team Building · Adversity Defeated/Fix My Life · Vision Boarding · Passion Purpose Paper

Rynette has spoken for

Schools · Youth empowerment and motivation seminars · Church Groups
Women's Conferences/Seminars · Correctional Facilities/Reformatory Institutes

Rynette can be booked for

Keynote · Hosting · Panel Discussions · Facilitator Breakout Sessions and More

ARE YOU READY!!!
Book Rynette for your next event
because your event deserves
a next level experience.
· ·

RYNETTESPEAKS.COM
· ·

Made in the USA
Middletown, DE
16 July 2019